27068092

5/09

DATE DUE

DEMCO 128-8155

JORDIN SPARKS

TAMARA ORR

Mitchell Lane
PUBLISHERS

P.O. Box 196
Hockessin, Delaware 19707
Visit us on the web: www.mitchelllane.com
Comments? email us: mitchelllane@mitchelllane.com

Mitchell Lane PUBLISHERS

Printing   1   2   3   4   5   6   7   8   9

A Robbie Reader
Contemporary Biography

Albert Pujols	Alex Rodriguez	Aly and AJ
Amanda Bynes	Ashley Tisdale	Brittany Murphy
Charles Schulz	Dakota Fanning	Dale Earnhardt Jr.
Donovan McNabb	Drake Bell & Josh Peck	Dr. Seuss
Dwayne "The Rock" Johnson	Dylan & Cole Sprouse	Eli Manning
Hilary Duff	Jamie Lynn Spears	Jessie McCartney
Johnny Gruelle	The Jonas Brothers	**Jordin Sparks**
LeBron James	Mia Hamm	Miley Cyrus
Miranda Cosgrove	Raven-Symone	Shaquille O'Neal
The Story of Harley-Davidson	Syd Hoff	Tiki Barber
Tom Brady	Tony Hawk	

Orr, Tamra.
  Jordin Sparks / by Tamra Orr.
      p. cm. — (A Robbie reader)
  Includes bibliographical references, discography, and index.
  ISBN 978-1-58415-727-4 (library bound)
  1. Sparks, Jordin—Juvenile literature. 2. Singers—United States—Juvenile literature. I. Title.
  ML3930.S712O77 2008
  782.42164092—dc22
  [B]
                                                        2008017003

ABOUT THE AUTHOR: Tamra Orr is the author of almost 150 nonfiction books for kids of all ages. She is also a real *American Idol* fan, even though she doesn't actually vote. Orr lives in the Pacific Northwest with her husband and four children (ages 24 to 12) and truly believes that being an author has to be the most wonderful job in the world.

TABLE OF CONTENTS

Chapter One
Reaching a Dream 5

Chapter Two
Getting Started 9

Chapter Three
Going to School 15

Chapter Four
Becoming an Idol 21

Chapter Five
Giving Back 25

Chronology 28
Discography 28
Find Out More 29
    Books and Magazine Articles 29
    Works Consulted 29
    On the Internet 30
Glossary 31
Index 32

Words in **bold** type can be found in the glossary.

The surprise and excitement of the moment is clear as Jordin Sparks and Blake Lewis wait to hear who has won the title of American Idol.

Reaching a Dream

Have you ever had a really big dream? Most people do. They may have to work a long time to reach it too. With Jordin Sparks, however, her dream came true when she was only seventeen years old.

On May 23, 2007, Jordin stood under the hot lights of the TV studio, with more than 30 million eyes on her from all over the country. After weeks and weeks of singing her very best on *American Idol*, the contest was down to just Blake Lewis and her.

"I had no idea what was going to happen," says Jordin. "When Blake and I were standing up there [waiting to hear who won], he was just like, 'I love you, sweetheart,' and he squeezed

Moments after being announced the American Idol winner and singing "This Is My Now," Jordin gives in to tears as she is surrounded by the other contestants from the season.

my hand and I realized that no matter what happened, everything was going to be OK."

The waiting was tough! "All of a sudden, Ryan [Seacrest], goes, 'The winner of *American Idol* . . . then he dragged it out, waited a couple of minutes before he said anything," recalls Jordin. "He said my name and I covered my face with my hands. I saw people clapping but I couldn't hear them. My heart was pounding so hard. It's one of those moments that I'll never, ever forget as long as I live."

Jordin was so surprised at winning that when Seacrest handed her the microphone, she blanked on the lyrics of the song she was supposed to sing. "He handed me the mike and I was like . . . uhhhhhh. And then the words just came out. I don't know how they did. They just did. . . . And seeing everybody there—my family was all bawling their eyes out—and my brother and my uncles."

It was truly an amazing moment for Jordin. It was one she had been hoping for since she was old enough to talk—or, in her case, sing.

Jordin gets a big hug from her #1 fan—her father and former pro football player Phillippi Sparks as they appear together on NBC's *Today* program in New York.

Getting Started

Jordin Brianna Sparks was born December 22, 1989, in Phoenix, Arizona. Her father, Phillippi Sparks, a former player for the New York Giants football team, is African American. Her mother, Jodi Wiedmann, is white. A few years after Jordin was born, the family was joined by her brother Phillippi Jr., or P.J.

From the age of eighteen months, Jordin loved to sing. Although she never took any real singing lessons, she kept getting better. "I used to put on my nicest dress and pretend that I was at an awards show," she remembers with a grin. "I would also blast my music as loud as I could and try to sing exactly like the person who was singing it."

Jordin recalls seeing *American Idol* for the first time and seeing Kelly Clarkson win. "I got a little choked up when I started singing the song because it's what I've always wanted to do," she says. "When I was twelve, I remember the show was just starting out. We were actually watching the **finale** and I was just like, 'I want to do that, Mom.' "

In 2002, Kelly Clarkson won first place on *American Idol*. She performed "A Moment Like This," a song that would later appear on her first album, *Thankful.* Her performance was a big inspiration for Jordin.

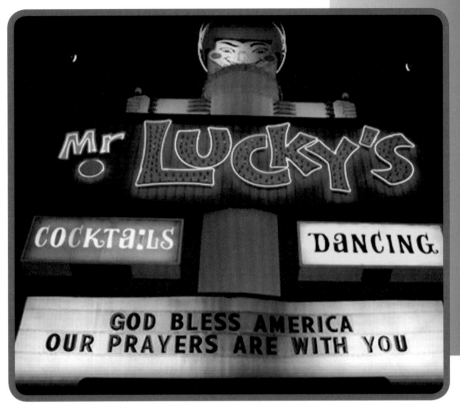

This local restaurant was one of the first places that Jordin sang in front of an audience. She made such a good impression that she was selected to record a CD with several other performers.

By thirteen, she started entering singing contests. Her voice surprised everyone! In 2002, Jordin won the Coca-Cola Rising Star contest. The following year, she won the Glendale Youth Fest Talent Show and other Arizona contests. She even joined other musicians and sang on a CD called *Live at Mr. Lucky's.*

Jordin kept winning awards. In 2004, she appeared on *America's Most Talented Kids* twice, winning once. She also took second place in the Music in the Rockies National Competition.

Every step of the way, Jordin's family was right there with her. "My family was always very loving, very grounded," Jordin explains. "My dad kept us calm . . . and my mom made me fiercely independent. She was big on teaching

From the first song, Jordin's family has been there to encourage and support her. Parents Phillippi and Jodi, along with brother P.J., join her at the Jordin Sparks Celebrity Charity Gala 2008 during Super Bowl XLII.

Along with becoming one of the nation's most popular singers, Jordin has also become a model for magazines. Her fashion style and happy personality act as inspiration for many young girls across the country.

us responsibility and fending for ourselves," she continues. "I think I understood early the importance of setting goals and being prepared to meet them."

Jordin had no idea that she'd be meeting one of her goals—becoming a singer the whole world would recognize—in just a few years.

Jordin takes a moment to sing a song at the Gibson booth during the 50th Annual Grammy Awards. Learning how to play the guitar has helped her to produce the music she loves so much.

Going to School

Jordin's parents wanted to do everything they could to help support their musical daughter. "With me or P.J. or any of the other kids in the family, [my parents] have been like, 'What do you love to do?' They'll say, 'Are you sure that's what you want? Okay, we'll help you get there,'" says Jordin. "I love to sing, so I got a guitar to help me with my music and broaden everything. They've just always been so supportive. It's so encouraging. I'm very lucky."

Although Jordin is **biracial**, she was never treated differently for it. "Amazingly, I never felt singled out," she shares. "Even at school, we were always treated with respect, never out of the ordinary, which when I look back," she adds, "is really an incredible thing. I try to be that accepting whenever I encounter a new or difficult situation."

What was Jordin like when she was in school? "I had braces and I had to wear headgear!" she recalls. "I loved my braces, actually. For me, they were like a piece of jewelry. Instead of the silver or **pewter**, I had gold braces. . . . I got to change the colors and stuff and I had the rubber bands."

Jordin went to a private Christian school for many years, and when she started going to public school, it was hard. "I was just in that **rebel** mode," she explains. "That was for about the first half of eighth grade, and then I thought, 'This is so dumb!' So I went back to being myself again."

When it came time for high school, Jordin went for two years to Sandra Day O'Connor in Glendale, but then she and her family decided to finish her

Along with Cameron Diaz and the Jonas Brothers, Jordin participated in the 21st Annual Nickelodeon Kids' Choice Awards Celebrity Burp-Off. Her belch made her laugh as much as the kids did!

schooling at home. That way she could spend more time doing what she loved most—singing.

It was a great decision too. Jordin was about to turn singing into her career—and her ticket to stardom.

17

A smiling Jordin prepares for her next performance on the *American Idol* stage.

Becoming an Idol

The trip to becoming an American Idol almost never happened. In 2006, at her first **audition** in Los Angeles, Jordin was sent home. "I remember being at that first audition looking down that long line that just seemed endless and asking myself, 'What am I bringing to this— how will they ever notice me?' " Being rejected was tough. "I went home, shook it off and said, 'Wait a minute. I can do this if they let me.' "

Jordin got a second chance. She auditioned again in Seattle, and this time, she made it. On February 21, 2007, she came out and sang "Gimme One Reason" by Tracy Chapman. Three months later, she sang "This Is My Now" and won the official title of *American Idol.*

Getting a rare second chance, Jordin was able to audition once again for *American Idol*. This time she won the judges over.

While she was involved in the competition, some reporters made less-than-kind comments about Jordin's figure and height. (She is six feet tall.) Her response? "Hollywood needs to get over it. My mom and my dad were always saying, 'You're beautiful, Jordin.' I'm really comfortable in my own skin." She adds, "I learned that I'm not ever going to be a size 2. I would look so weird as a size 2. . . . It just wouldn't be healthy."

Pam Wiedmann, Jordin's grandmother, saw how much winning *American Idol* helped Jordin. "I think it really helped boost her self-esteem and made her realize she's beautiful as she is," she says. "It was huge to see her confidence level grow. . . . She's standing taller now."

In 2006, Jordin discovered Torrid, a store in many malls that carries clothing in sizes 12 and up. "They have clothes for girls who aren't an average size so they can totally feel cute and flirty and still keep up with the latest trends," says Jordin. Later, she did a modeling shoot for Torrid clothes in *Seventeen* magazine.

Listening to the judges' comments can sometimes be the hardest part of performing on *American Idol*. Jordin always managed to smile—even when it was time for Simon Cowell's (left) sometimes brutal remarks. Paula Abdul's (middle) and Randy Jackson's (right) comments were usually easier to hear.

As a model and spokesperson for Torrid, Jordin signs autographs for the chain's employees. Jordin has helped young girls all across the country feel comfortable with being taller or bigger than the typical female celebrity.

Jordin's life has been just one long dream come true. She was singing on TV. The world knew her face and voice. What more could the future hold?

When Jordin sang at Super Bowl XLII, it brought together two of her biggest passions—music and football. Her father came to watch her perform at the University of Phoenix Stadium in Arizona.

Giving Back

With a professional football player for a dad, Jordin grew up loving the game. One thing she had always dreamed of doing was singing the national anthem at a Super Bowl game. She had already sung for the Phoenix Suns, the Arizona Cardinals, and the Arizona Diamondbacks. Then it happened—she was asked to sing for the 2008 Super Bowl.

"I can't believe they asked me to do it," says Jordin. ". . . Millions of people watch *American Idol* . . . I didn't think anything could get any bigger. Now I'm doing the Super Bowl and billions of people are watching that."

After her big win on *American Idol*, Jordin released her first album. Since then, she has worked hard to help others. In October 2007, Jordin, along with celebrities Jessica Alba, Vanessa Williams, Katharine McPhee, Carrie Underwood, and Reba McEntire, designed jackets sold on eBay. The profits went to support SOS Children's Villages.

In 2008, she went to Ghana, a country in Africa, along with President and Mrs. George

Jordin was thrilled to get the chance to perform the national anthem for President George W. Bush and the First Lady at the American Embassy in Accra, Ghana, in February 2008.

W. Bush. They were there to help remind the world to fight **malaria** in Africa. Malaria is a deadly disease carried by mosquitoes. "Traveling to Ghana with Malaria No More gives me the incredible opportunity to see for myself what a difference a simple mosquito net can make in the life of a child," says Jordin. "I'm so proud of the millions of *American Idol* fans who helped save lives through last year's Idol Gives Back. I hope that my own fans will learn along with me as I discover more about this **devastating** (DEH-vuh-stay-ting) disease and the simple steps we can all take to make Malaria No More."

By the age of seventeen, Jordin had achieved more than many people three times older than she. She has important advice for young people. "Try to just love yourself for you and who you are, and people will love you once that gets started. Because once you start to love yourself, there's kind of a light around you that people see. Even if it's just the tiniest bit of confidence . . . [people] will want to get to know you. . . . Just try being yourself," she says. "Just keep trying!"

CHRONOLOGY

1989 Jordin Brianna Sparks is born on December 22 in Phoenix, Arizona.

2002 She wins the Coca-Cola Rising Star competition.

2003 She wins the Glendale Youth Fest Talent Show; releases extended-play version of the song "For Now."

2004 Performs on a compilation album called *Live at Mr. Lucky's*.

2006 She auditions for *American Idol* in Los Angeles and Seattle; wins Colgate Country Showdown in Arizona.

2007 On March 8, she makes it into the top 24 on *American Idol*. Her album *Jordin Sparks* is released. On May 23, she wins *American Idol*. She participates in a benefit for SOS Children's Villages.

2008 She sings the national anthem in the Super Bowl in February. She travels to Ghana for Malaria No More. She releases a video for her new single "One Step At A Time." "No Air," her duet with Chris Brown, lands in the Top 5. She tours with Alicia Keys.

DISCOGRAPHY

2007 *Jordin Sparks*

2004 *Live at Mr. Lucky's*
(compilation)

2003 "For Now" (EP)

FIND OUT MORE

Books and Magazine Articles

Brown, Anastasia. *Make Me a Star: Industry Insiders Reveal How to Make It in Music.* Nashville, Tennessee: Thomas Nelson Publishers, 2008.

Canfield, Jack, and Mark Victor Hansen. *Chicken Soup for the American Idol Soul: Stories from the Idols and their Fans that Open Your Heart and Make Your Soul Sing.* Deerfield Beach, Florida: HCI Books, 2007.

US Weekly, *Entertainment Weekly June 2007 Jordin Sparks Entertainment Weekly*, 2007.

Works Consulted

American Idol '07. "Jordin Sparks: Just Your Average Teen." *People*, May, 25, 2007. http://www.people.com/people/package/americanidol2007/article/0,,20007868_20040421,00.html Accessed May 30, 2008.

Fuoco-Karasinski, Christina. "Live Daily Interview: Jordin Sparks." *TV Guide.* www.tvguide.com/news/american-idol-jordin/070711-01. Accessed March 20, 2008.

Hensley, Dennis. "Jordin Sparks Is Living Out Her Dream." *MSNBC.* www.msnbc.msn.com/id/21918021/print/1/displaymode/1098/. Accessed March 20, 2008.

Malcom, Shawna. "American Idol's Jordin 'I Can't Believe That I Won!' " *TV Guide.* http://www.tvguide.com/News-Views/Interviews-Features/Article/default.aspx?posting=%7B152F66A3-EAF6-4D91-94BB-3F5401F72C17%7D. Accessed March 20, 2008.

Rizzo, Monica. "Jordin Sparks: I Like My Curves." *People.* http://www.people.com/people/article/0,,20040649,00.html. Accessed March 20, 2008.

FIND OUT MORE

Schneider, Shari. "Celebrities, Including Jordin Sparks, Jessica Alba, Eric Dane, Will Help Charity Auction on eBay." PR News Wire. http://www.associatedcontent. com/article/387283/celebrities_including_jordin_sparks. html. Accessed April 6, 2008.

Unknown. "Biography." Jordin Sparks. http://www. jordinsparks.com/biography. Accessed March 20, 2008.

Unknown. "It's My Life." PBS Kids. http://pbskids.org/ itsmylife/celebs/interviews/jordin.html. Accessed March 20, 2008.

Unknown. "Jordin 'Sparks' an Interest in Fighting Malaria in Africa." Malaria No More Press Release. February 19, 2008.

Zepeda, Dana Meltzer. "On Tour with American Idol: The Jordin Sparks Q and A." *TV Guide.* http://www.tvguide. com/News/american-idol-jordin/070711-01. Accessed March 20, 2008.

On the Internet

American Idol: Jordin Sparks http://www.americanidol.com/ contestants/season6/jordin_sparks/

Jordin Sparks Fan Club
http://www.jordin-online.com/

Jordin Sparks Official Web Site
http://www.jordinsparks.com/

GLOSSARY

audition (aw-DIH-shun)—A tryout for a part in a play, television show, or movie.

biracial (by-RAY-shul)—Having parents from different races, such as black and white.

devastating (DEH-vuh-stay-ting)—Completely ruining.

finale (fih-NAA-lee)—The last scene in a show, or the last show in a series.

malaria (muh-LAYR-ee-uh)—A disease carried by mosquitoes that causes high fever and sometimes death.

pewter (PYOO-tur)—A metal that contains tin and sometimes lead.

rebel (REH-bul)—Someone who acts against parents, government, or any other form of rule.

INDEX

Abdul, Paula 22

Alba, Jessica 26

American Idol 4, 5, 6, 10, 18, 19, 20, 21, 22, 23, 25, 27

America's Most Talented Kids 12

Bush, George W. 26–27

Bush, Laura 26–27

Chapman, Tracy 19

Clarkson, Kelly 10

Coca-Cola Rising Star contest 11

Cowell, Simon 22

Diaz, Cameron 17

Glendale Youth Fest Talent show 11

Grammy Awards 14

Jackson, Randy 22

Jonas Brothers 17

Kids' Choice Awards 17

Kodak Theater 4, 6

Lewis, Blake 4, 5

Live at Mr. Lucky's 11

McEntire, Reba 26

McPhee, Katharine 26

Malaria No More 27

Mr. Lucky's 11

Music in the Rockies National Competition 12

Nickelodeon Kids' Choice Awards 17

Seacrest, Ryan 7

Seventeen magazine 21

SOS Children's Villages 26

Sparks, Jordin
    album by 25
    appearance of 21
    auditions 18, 19, 20
    birth of 9
    and charities 12, 26–27
    childhood of 9–13, 15–17
    in contests 11, 12
    education of 15, 16–17
    at Grammy Awards 14
    heritage of 9, 15
    in magazines 13, 21
    winning *American Idol* 5, 6, 26

Sparks, Phillippi (father) 7, 8, 9, 12, 15, 24, 25

Sparks, Phillippi, Jr. (P.J., brother) 7, 8, 9, 12, 15

Super Bowl XLII 12, 24, 24, 25

Torrid 21, 23

Underwood, Carrie 26

Wiedmann, Jodi (mother) 7, 8, 9, 12, 15

Wiedmann, Pam (grandmother) 21

Williams, Vanessa 26